To Kathy

Memoirs

from

Down

in the

Boondocks

A Spiritual Journey through

Poem and Short Story

BY

KATE INGRID PAUL

Many Blessings,

Kate Paul

MEMOIRS FROM DOWN IN THE BOONDOCKS:
A SPIRITUAL JOURNEY THROUGH POEM
AND SHORT STORY

FIRST EDITION

ISBN-13: 978-1493576548
ISBN-10: 1493576542

I am ever grateful for my friends and teachers in the flesh and in spirit, and my friends and teachers in written word... in the words and stories and poetry that have inspired me and continue to remind me of who I am.

The grandest adventures are those of the heart.
Indeed, they are the only pursuits worth having.

A note from the author

I've never been one to write 'proper' poetry. I rarely color within the lines of verse and meter and rhyme. Poetry at its heart is an expression of the heart. It is an outward manifestation, using words to paint a picture, of what is inscribed on the heart and soul of the one holding the pen. It is an expression of the beauty that is felt coursing through everything in existence. It is a way to connect, ever more, with Divine truth. Never once have I felt that I write poetry; but rather, through me, it writes itself. And as the words come through my hand, I am healed... and so may you too find joy and healing in these words that are meant for this Grand World.

~Kate

Contents

Full Circle

Introduction 1

The Spiral Path

A Dream of Awakening 23

Divine Love

On Men, Birds, and a Broken Record 63

The Journey to Wholeness

Spirit Waves 99

Full

Circle

Introduction

I grew up on the Mesabi Iron Range in Northeastern Minnesota, a land peppered with taconite mining operations laid out like a mosaic atop the rich deposits of the Biwabik Iron Formation. A land where tiered waste rock stockpiles and red dirt roads embody a special kind of beauty. A land where the forests and lakes are rich with people who appreciate them. A land where thirty below zero is not only expected, but a bragging point as well. It is also a place where a somewhat eclectic subculture exists; one where alcoholism is touted as social drinking, narrow-mindedness is a virtue of passion, and chauvinism still lurks as an evident undercurrent. But in this place are also the people nearest and dearest to my heart... many are the most noble, accepting, and generous people you could possibly meet, and they would do anything for a friend or neighbor in need.

In general, rugged individualism abounds here perhaps much like it did in the wild lands of the west. This, after all, was virtually raw frontier land only 130 years ago when my great-grandpa came from Norway to seek out a new life. Very little came easy, and for the men and women who broke fresh ground here... to log, or farm, or work in the first treacherous underground iron ore mines, they had to be tough and resilient, they had to be of single-mindedness and hold their ground in order to survive; but they also needed each other in order to be truly successful. So it appears that their demeanors... the good and the bad, take it as you may, still proudly persist in the culture that they helped create. And even though I was raised here, "Down in the Boondocks," as my grandma used to say, I still experience culture shock on occasion; but I have come to see this as endearing, and it is indeed anything except boring.

I left this place after high school to seek a dream of a more diverse world, one where perhaps I could find a job and make a life for myself that was not tied to the ups and downs of a fickle economy driven by the global demand for steel, but was tied instead to my passions and interests. After a 17-year absence, I was drawn back to this place by a different kind of dream... one where a slower-paced life closer to the land would allow me to be myself and to rediscover my lost and hidden passions. I was delighted to discover that in many ways this place was even more wondrous than I remembered from childhood... it has a spirit that knows me well and I, in turn, have come to know it as an ancient and wise friend... one that helped guide and teach me as a child, and continues to do so.

My journey away from my childhood home and back again is metaphorical in a way to my spiritual journey away from myself and back again. That they also coincide in time and space is not coincidental, but my testament that life is not just a sum of its parts, but a whole and endless experience intertwined in ways that can only be described as magical. No matter how you take it apart or break it down into timelines of individual experiences and lessons learned, the puzzle pieces we remember are never separate from the whole... and the whole can be found fully intact within each piece. Everything is woven together; when we take a step back from any situation, this is the knowingness that slips in. In the greater picture, there is a clear vision of our wholeness, and within this vision we find pure choice. We discover that the journey is really about taking the next step, and that next step is happening right now... and we are choosing it for ourselves this very moment.

These are my notes... my memoirs. They are the puzzle pieces... the stories, poetry, and thoughts that I have written down since I have been living back home on the Iron Range... Down in the Boondocks. They are an inseparable part of a greater whole, and my hope is that these pieces will remind you of the wholeness and holiness of life in which each of us are intimately entwined...

My Love Affair

I am thankful for divine inspiration
That lives in every molecule of air I breathe,
That upwells in every feeling flowing through me,
That dances on my rooftop,
That runs naked through the woods
And howls at the moon,
That others have labeled crazy and silly and strange;
But a name cannot be given
To something this wild and free...

And I don't care.
I don't care what the world thinks
About this love affair of mine.
It fills me with joy and hope and desire overflowing...

And we'll make love...
And conceive of dreams
No one has ever dared dream before...

And then give birth
To a world worth living in.

The Spaces Between

Life is a mixture of bitter and sweet.

Don't shake things so hard
That you mix them up.

Let them be what they are,
And let them pass as they may.

Be grateful for both, but cling to neither;

For your true joy dwells in the spaces between.

Scattered

I've scattered myself like dust in the wind,
I've blown around; I've been spread too thin.
My attention pulled in a thousand different ways,
My love blocked out by the monotony of days.

Life has been dull, listless, and tattered,
My heart has been bruised, beaten, and shattered.

But I tell you, dear soul, that none of this matters...

When I stop the lies and the judgments unfold,
I see the truth standing so bold,
Holding its hand out, offering this token...

The love I need I already have,

My heart is whole...
It never was broken.

Now I scatter myself like stars in the sky,
The love in my heart soars that high,
Then rains back down with lightning and thunder,
Satiating your heart, never broken asunder.

Dear Moon

Dear Moon,
Bathe me in your precious light,
Fill my heart with all possibilities,
As I dream of warmer days
And sweet union with my beloved;

As I dream of greater ways to be in this world,
Suddenly, I become;
I become what I already am...
And I am complete...

Your light reminding me
Of the pathways already lit inside me,
Leading me back to myself
Time and time again.

The Path

I see I have a purpose here.
I have a special place among the stars,
Where I am at once ONE with all that exists,
Yet very much ME,

With the full-brunt of all the life force
In the universe
Pulsing through me...
Setting me aglow...
Setting me free.

And it's a bit like walking in the dark...
I can't see the path,
But I know it

By the feeling.

Dirt, Rain, and Sun

The rows of cabbage don't yet know
What will happen.
Feet in the muck and rain coming down,
Do they know what miracles will come?

They don't worry, like I do,
About the weather or woes,
Most of which never come as forecasted.

They eat dirt, drink rain, and soak up the sun;
Not knowing the end or the beginning,
They just grow and grow and grow.

I know not of these too;
But I do know something wild and true...

Dirt, rain, and sun
Are where miracles are sown,
And dreams do sprout anew.

The Frog Chorus

The forest came alive tonight
With the deafening sound
Of frog chorus;

And my heart starts to sing
A primal song
Filled with hope
And continuance.

Summer's End

As crickets sing near summers end,
I can see that everything is dying;
The plants that bloom to produce their fruit,
Bloom harder and quicker under stress.

I see their beauty as I roam field and wood,
Reminding me there is more than what I see,
There is more that I can be,
As I taste this mystery...

And what is worth fighting for?
Your breath against death?
Yes, yes... and that is all,
Because when summer dies to fall,
Her warm breath turns cold;

And I'll light a fire in her honor.

Soaring

I saw a bird-of-prey soaring high above;
I mean, really high up.
It looked like he was touching the clouds.

It's not migration season,
and it certainly wasn't hunting from way up there.
There's a lot of energy in the air.
The sun is shining hot and the sky is filled
with those big, billowy pre-storm clouds.

I bet it's cooler up there next to the clouds.
I bet it feels good to be that high above the ground
with wings outstretched; every muscle in tip-top shape
and poised to follow the will of the traveler.

You couldn't convince me that there's any other
reason to be up there other than for the pure,
exhilarating joy of it;

The pure, unequivocal
"Why not, because I can" of it.
And how many choose instead to stay close
to the ground?
How many, how many...

Fresh Wings

Crawling on the ground,
With wings bruised and torn,
A butterfly appeared to be near his end.
When I reached down to touch him,
He took perfect flight, as if on fresh wings...

Regardless of outer appearances,
Regardless of what appears bruised and torn,
Regardless of who tries to tamper with us,

The soul is like that...
Always on fresh wings.

Hunting

Tonight I am hunting.
I am going out to hunt for God;
Under stars and moonlight,
I gently step upon the earth.

And if I am quiet enough,
If I am still and silent enough,
He will come into my sight,
Offering Himself to me.

His body nourishing mine,
I become HIS trophy.
This hunter becomes the beautiful hunted,
Gladly surrendering my fate.

What Poets Know

Poets know
We write for ourselves,
We sing for ourselves;
For the joy, for the pain,
For nothing is in vain.

We write for the journey,
And sing ourselves to sleep,
We dance like crazy bastards
On rooftops
Below our feet,

And toss out golden lassos
Towards the moon
And a zillion beaming stars;
To catch a moonbeam
Or perhaps some starlight
Filled with words for our jar...
Then watch them play like
Fireflies.

We write for the love,
We write for the hate,
We write and we write
Till there's nothing left to abate,
Till there's nothing left but scars...
And then we write about those
Too.

Heart fire

Where rain falls on the thirsty earth,
Lightning flashes across the sky.
On the ground, lightening bugs are flying high;
Like lovers with beacons,
Calling each other home,
Heart fires ablaze.

I stand and I watch, anticipating;
I listen with ears and heart open,
Waiting for wisdom to come heed my beacon,
Calling her home
With my heart fire ablaze.

Merry-go-round

We are all just temporary passengers
On this beautiful, blue globe;

Spinning around and around and around,
Like riders on a merry-go-round;

Saying, "Yes, yes,
Let's do it again!"

The

Spiral

Path

A Dream of Awakening

I grew up paying close attention to the land. I felt as though the land spoke to me, and I listened with my heart open, as children do. In the woods that surrounded my childhood home, I could always find a myriad of adventures calling out to me from the land. There were places that called me to run and play, those that called me to build creative shelters, and those that called me to just be still and watch the beauty of life unfold around me; there were also places that called out a warning... "Be careful... stay away." I listened to it all, without pausing to think much about it or to question the messages I received; I was too busy following my joy and having fun in my yard and the surrounding forest.

From a very early age, I developed a deep fascination with the history of the land I lived on. While rummaging through the laundry room junk drawer one day, I found an old arrowhead made out of a dense, dark-colored rock. It was cool to the touch, but warmed in my hands as I caressed the smooth, dark surface filled with worn-down notches created from the flaking and shaping process. When I asked my mom about it, she informed me that my dad found it nearby while they were breaking ground for the house several years prior. I felt an instant affinity with this piece of rock... Someone had taken the time to carefully carve this tool for a great purpose... to feed and clothe themselves and their family... to survive here, to live a life and thrive here, on this very land upon which I now lived. This rock held deep secrets; I could sense it. And I had a great desire to know those secrets... to hear the stories of the people who carved it.

I also grew up paying close attention to my dreams. I would often have extremely vivid dreams, some of which were lucid, giving me conscious control while engaged in them. My dream world and my waking world would sometimes meld together; my mind being so immersed at a deeper level of consciousness that it frightened me at times. My most vivid dreams from childhood continue to live in my memories. One dream in particular, I will never forget. It was a dream I had on many nights, and it always began in the same way. I would awaken in my bed to the beating of drums coming from my back yard, just outside my bedroom wall. The sound was deep, rich, and ancient; the rhythm mesmerizing and persistent. It called to me and I was very curious, but my fears, which were greater than my curiosity, kept me in the house within the safety and warmth of my bed. I would wake up on other nights to the same drumming, the same alluring sounds calling me to come outside. I could sense the people who made the sounds, and I knew they wanted me to join them... They were the people of the arrowhead. This was my opportunity to see them, to meet them, and to perhaps have my desires fulfilled and learn secrets long hidden... to learn something of their story. After many, many nights, I finally grew brave enough to leave the comfort of my bed. I began to slowly and carefully walk down the hallway toward the stairway that led to the front door. Each night I woke up to the drumming, I would progress a little further down the hallway. I felt as if I was being tested, and I wondered if I would have enough courage to finally complete the journey and go outside to face this mystery.

Finally, one night, bolder than usual, I found my feet upon the cold, tile floor in the entryway at the front of the house, my hand grasping the doorknob. I quietly and gently turned it, and then stepped outside into the cool, dark air; but I didn't feel cold, my head reeling and my heart racing as my bare feet touched the soft earth in the yard. It was then I saw them, waiting for me... they were dressed in beautiful, elaborate, ceremonial-like attire that was no doubt reserved for special occasions. They were vibrant, joyful spirits, drumming and dancing to ancient rhythms that grew louder and louder as I walked closer. A woman approached me, hand outstretched, motioning me to join them. My fears dissolved and were quickly replaced with fascination and excitement. I began to dance with them, and I felt the rhythms resonating deep within me. Soon, my entire being was resonating with an intensely bright light and I felt the most exquisite joy I've ever experienced. I felt connected to these beautiful souls and with everything in existence in the Universe. I knew that THIS is what is possible; THIS is the feeling of LIFE, of ME, of GOD... THIS is who I AM... This light, this energy, this amazing feeling. It was like coming home to my rightful place in the world. This is where I belonged. Welcome home... welcome home.

I never spoke of my dream to anyone during my childhood. Somehow I knew that at best it would be brushed aside as "just a dream", and at worst I feared that others would think I was crazy. I felt that these spirits who came to me were my ancestors... that I had walked with them here before, on this very land. But regardless of whether this is so or not, I knew they were unequivocally a part of my spirit family, and once I became consciously aware of them, I felt supported and guided and protected in a way that I had not felt before.

Most of my vivid dreams stopped as I transitioned from childhood into my teenage years. It is no coincidence that this was also a point in my life when I began to spend less time with the land and more time with other concerns. I immersed myself in trying to fit into a junior high school subculture that was seemingly unforgiving... I became so concerned about what others thought about me, that I hardly noticed the transition I made from listening with my heart, to listening with fear and worry. I became obsessed with acting the right way, dressing the right way, and being the kind of person who would win the admiration of others. My main desire was to be okay in the eyes of others; I wanted their approval, their attention, and their good graces. I quickly forgot that I had never been anything other than okay. In fact, I was more than okay; but the journey back to this realization, and back to myself, took quite some time.

Well into adulthood, I found myself trudging through many of the fears that formed the basis of my self-consciousness and my need to be accepted by others at my own expense. In my struggles to be who I thought I needed to be, I became disconnected and lost. I feared letting go... even letting go of my struggles. How would I then define myself? I feared that letting go would mean disappearing, and my life would mean nothing. Not wanting to live any longer with these fears, I began working on shedding the false layers of my personality... layers that I built up over the years in my attempt to "fit in" and be "okay." Through this process, I began to experience a re-awakening to myself.

On one occasion, after partaking in a ceremony which focused on celebrating my true self, I found myself once again in the presence of the same spirits that visited me in my childhood dream. As in our first reunion, they welcomed me home... They spoke to me and told me that my HOME is in my HEART... my SACRED HEART... and no matter where I am on this earth or in my life, I am ALWAYS home. There is nothing I need to DO to become myself, as I am already there. I then began to experience that when I let go... when I let go of my struggles and my fears and my worries; when I let go of past hurts and my beliefs about how I think things should be, I don't disappear, I become... I become what I already am. And what I am is perfect, even with all my perceived imperfections. I am then able to see the perfection in everything, like looking through God's eyes at myself and the whole world, with unconditional love and acceptance for all of creation.

Now I often feel like the child I once was... beholding the wonder before me with an open heart. But I have something else too... a deeper understanding and appreciation for my own life and the life that surrounds me. And I see that this entire life is not unlike a dream. A beautiful, lucid, vivid dream wherein I play a pivotal role in what happens next... through where I focus my attention and what I think about. What others think about me is a part of their dream, not mine. In my dream, I get to choose to live from my heart and feel the vibrancy and the intense joy that originates from there...

This is Home... Welcome Home.

Heaven's Doorway

More often now I sit in Heaven's doorway...

Just to let the wind kiss me,
Just to let the stars sing to me,

And just to hear the spirits say
"You're home, you're home, you're home."

Don't wait

I made a wish in the open night air,
And a streak of light flashed across the sky.

"Don't wait for one of us to fall,
Before you speak of your desires.
Don't wait on the moon to rise above the treetops,
Before basking in its full beauty.
Don't wait to feel the peace of your divinity,
Before you embrace it.

Nothing is waiting on you.
You're already full.
You're already there."

I tell you this

I tell you this:
Don't get too complacent!
Don't get too comfortable
In your routine,
In the ruts you've worn with your body and mind.

I tell you this:
There is a restless traveler living deep in your soul...
Let him out!
Let her explore the spaces between your thoughts,
Let him traverse the distance
Between your mind and your heart,
Let her sing to you of melodies long forgotten,
Let him out, let him out!

I tell you this:
There is a landscape within you
As vast as the Universe;
Don't let it go unexplored!
There lie new discoveries
That only you can make.

Philosophy

You don't need great knowledge or
great philosophical concepts.

You don't need the acceptance of others.

You express your own divinity by
being alive and by
Loving yourself and others.

My Temple

My body is a temple.
It is the vehicle through which God expresses
God on Earth.

I am that expression
Of Love
Of Light

Of pure devotion to
The Way.

Making Love with the Sun

Sunlit rays move deep into my body,
Penetrating every cell, every molecule,
Growing hotter and brighter;
Awaking what lies dormant.

Waking up, waking up
Is the light and heat within;
Bursting out as hot and bright as the sun,
To make love with the world.

Belief

Limiting beliefs make for a limiting life.
Examine EVERY belief you have about
EVERYTHING.

Question every one of them,
Then ask yourself, "Does this belief serve me?"
If it does not serve you, or limits you,
Or does not feel right in your heart,
Release it...
Let it go.

There is nothing binding you
To your thoughts and beliefs about things,
Except for your own limiting perception.

Let go...
Spread the wings of your mind
And soar above your old ways of thinking
And being in this world.

You are born anew in each moment
Into the person you choose to be.

Helium

Lightness comes when you drop the heavy.
What makes something heavy are your
Thoughts about it.

Helium will spring from lead...
If you allow wisdom to reside in your head.

Think about that.

Ride the wind

Listen...
A voice calls on the wind,

"Come... Come... Drop the facade,
And come.
You haven't even begun to live,
So come...

Take your spirit and ride the wind...
Twirling and twisting,
Twisting and twirling,
Up and up and up."

Crossroads

I've walked a path
Swollen with possibilities,
Littered with good intentions
And the ever pervasive potholes of lost hope.

I've taken many turns
To see what lay around the bend,
What colors, sounds, and pictures lend,
To time long lost from start to end.

I traveled far from place to place,
I watched and I listened,
But I never could keep pace

With what I thought was destiny,
With what I knew of life for me,
Was hardly life, by means I gained,
As my only life is hardly sane.

So I stand again at a crossroads,
Seeing more and more clearly this day,
The direction is no longer as important
As the love I give along the way.

You were here

My ache is nothing compared to your annihilation,
Yet you stand there so peaceful and calm,
Forever giving, forever forgiving.

You are my brother, my sister,
The same source nourishes us all.
Everything... everything is a part of you,
You are a part of me.
Nothing... nothing exists alone...

Our spirits entwined,
Death and birth appear in the same doorway,
And become dance partners,
Teaching us to be light on our feet;
Teaching us to live and let go,
But never forget.

Forever grateful I stand before you...
I will not forget.
I will not forget...

You were here.

Standing Strong

Arms reaching up, up, up.
What are the secrets you hold up
To the heavens?

What are the stories you've seen,
Through autumn gale and winter snow,
Through lightning and thunder,
When strong winds blow,
Through rain and drought...

And in all my doubt,
Never once did you question,
Never once have you been
Anything but faithful,

Standing strong
And solid within.

Now

The future truly doesn't exist,
And neither does the past, really.

It's all a series of nows;
So there is now, and then there is now,
And before you know it,
It's now.
That's it...

So embrace it.
Embrace it with all of your heart,
Because it is all there ever is, ever was,
And ever will be.

It is now,
And in it, you decide how powerful you are
By focusing fully on this moment;
Or diffuse your power with the fiction you create,
When you wait
For something else.

The thrill of the ride

Life is like a river...
Sometimes wide and deep,
With gently moving waters
Full of quiet and peace;

Sometimes like the rapids,
Whitewater foam in your face,
Moving fast and furious
With no sign of a slower pace.

So just remember to cherish those times
Of gentle, of deep, of slow;

And never ever forget,
When you're hanging on tight
And fear letting go
In the peril of your fight...

Throw your hands in the air,
Feel the thrill of the ride,
Let the river be your guide...

For you've chosen this too.

Smoke and Mirrors

There are those of us who live our entire lives
Embedded in the masks
That push and pull
Like the strings of a marionette.

Five dollars a show,
Come sit and watch,
While they dance and prance
And vie for your glance.

They so love to lure you
Up onto the stage,
To be drugged and dazed
In a comfortable, conformable haze.

Drama so seductive
It plays off your pain and your fears,
But in the shadow of your true light,
It all turns to smoke and mirrors.

Superglue

Oh my, oh my, how we love to wear
These masks that I would so love to tear
Right off your face so you can see
That you are you, and I am me.

But I cannot do this work for you,
The masks are stuck like superglue,
And the only way for you to begin
Is to let them go and shed your skin.

See them all for what they are,
You've used them to cover wounds and scars,
But the only thing they ever hide
Is the love and truth that dwell inside.

Remind Me

All things happen in good time;
So remind me why time flies,
Or stands still.
Remind me of the ways
To be motionless in chaos,
And move gracefully
Through the silence
That echoes through my heart.

U Turns

Sometimes, in seeking the truth,
We find harsh things.
Sometimes, in moving toward the light,
We pass through darkness.
Sometimes, when seeking the best in people,
We encounter the worst.
Sometimes, the road isn't clear,
But we move ahead anyway,
We move through both night and day,
And discover
Regardless of how it looks
Or what others say,
Or how we feel about it
On any particular day,
It is our path,
Our chosen way;
For we are travelers here
In God's land,
And there is no One Way,
Wrong Way,
No Passing Zone...
And U Turns are OK.

Becoming

I am becoming...

Like the flower that becomes the fruit,
Like the fruit that births the seed,
And the seed becomes new growth;

I am becoming

Just

Like

That.

Silent Journey

Who listens when we talk?
For our day to day words
Write the story of our lives.

Who hears what we think about?
The dreams and dream breakers,
The sweet and the bitter
That drip like sticky dew
Upon our minds,
Like water on fertile ground.

Who feels our emotions?
Rushing through like changing weather,
Storming by, then peaceful calm;
A sudden joy, a disturbing qualm.

Who hears us when we grieve?
Or when we pray for sunny weather;
When we can't make up our minds,
When we want for something better.

Every word, the noisy and the quiet,
Even a silent thought
Are all written here,
Everything is heard;
Every thought, every deed,
Every word.

Like footprints left in soft, bare earth,
We leave our stories behind;
We take our hearts divine,
And move on and move on...

You're an open book, my friend;
And like a beautiful, beautiful song,
You sing throughout eternity,
Ever poignant and strong...

Your every word touches everything else...
What legacy hath you belong?

God's traveling show

Ahhh, Judgment,
Sweet, sweet, sweet
Judgment;
Who are you, really?

I can't hate you,
Nor can I adore you,
For I'd rather you not
Stick around.

However, you seem so attached to me,
So... oh, how shall I say it?
So much like an organ I don't need,
But have come to believe I do.

You created this ruler
I carry in my pocket,
And hold up to everyone I see;
And say, "You are too much of this,
Not enough of that,
Too skinny,
Too smart,
Too stupid,
Too fat."

Oh good grief, Judgment!
Don't be so harsh
About things you don't know;

What you see,
You see, is all a part of
God's traveling show.

I AM

It isn't about creating a stress-free, peaceful life
By trying to control the situations around you.
You can only move the furniture around so much,
And avoid to some degree those people and things
That drag you down.

What it's about is BEING peace,
So that when chaos ensues and others try to impose
Their poisonous drama onto you,
You are unmoved,
You are at peace;
Because when you see past the unserving beliefs
And self-defeating thoughts,
Peace is what YOU ARE.

THIS is the calm within the storm,
The great movement without moving,
That moves mountains and splits seas;

The loud, blatant secret...

I AM.

Beauty

There is a beauty that cannot be seen,
But only felt with the heart.

It rides the winds, hidden from our groggy view,
As we go through each day,
Busying ourselves
With the common work before us.

Sometimes I feel it caressing my cheek,
Blowing me kisses,
And whispering in my ear...

"Follow your heart, follow your bliss,
Feel the pull of your heart's desires...
Let them dance on the wind."

Oh, how I love to spend time in the presence
Of this mystical, mischievous friend
Who would make love to me all day if I allowed.

Divine Hands

I think I had a hard time
Settling into this body;
Sometimes I look at this hand
And think,
"This can't be mine."

Yet I have come to be
Quite attached
To this form,
And fear that losing it
Would mean losing myself;
How funny that is.

Ahhh... If we took more time
To gaze upon
These divine hands of ours,
We might just find the answers
We seek;

And come to realize
The infinite,
Creative force
We can be.

Mermaids

I believe in mermaids,
Because I believe in magic and mystery
And magnificent creatures
That don't need our eyes to exist.

The world is full of beauty unseen,
Full of hidden wonders;
But if only we look into our hearts,
Suddenly we see
With the eyes of mystery,
And majesty;

And a whole new world appears,
Where we can sense those
Who have been hidden.

Star People

We are star people
Burning hot and bright,

We are our darkness,
And we are the light.

We are the pathways
That we each seek,

In ancient rhythm,
We keep the beat

Of every heart
Of every breath
Of every movement
Of life and death.

The Whole Show

I stood watching and listening to the rain
For a long time tonight.
It was serene and peaceful and cleansing.

And then, as the rain started to let up,
The fireflies came out to dance...

Reminding me
That there is always more beauty to experience
If I am patient enough to stay

For the whole show.

Divine

Love

On Men, Birds, and a Broken Record

I developed a dysfunctional relationship with men early in life. By the age of two or three, I was already "in love" with a neighbor boy... and there began an interesting phenomenon. Obsessive thoughts about him and fantasies about someday being married to him began playing over and over in my head like a broken record skipping on the turntable. This boy continued to spin around and round in my head throughout my childhood. Eventually, he was replaced by other boys, but somebody's face was always on this broken record. In my teenage years, the repetitive fantasies of being swept off my feet were replaced more and more with stories of heartache. They'd repeat over and over in my mind, and I'd re-live the scenes, the rejection, and the pain. Like a chronic case of obsessive-compulsive disorder, I became a prisoner to this insane game where I continued to be disappointed again and again, because real life could never live up to the fairytales in my mind. I believed that my ultimate happiness depended on having a happy ending with a man.

Feeling incomplete, I needed something to hold on to, and the agony of a lost love or an unrequited love became a substitute for the love itself. At least I wasn't alone... I had my agony and the memory of some guy, spinning around in my head... a companion nonetheless, even if bad company.

On the other hand, I developed a relationship with Ovenbirds at an appropriate time during my life. These drab-colored, but brightly spirited warblers bring back memories from childhood and the woods that surround the house I grew up in. Their loud voices singing, "TEAcher-TEAcher-TEAcher" overpower other sounds in the forest, making it easy to pick them out of the crowd. They build their little dome-shaped "Dutch oven" style nests tucked into the leaves and debris on the forest floor. I got to know this charismatic little bird well during my first season doing field work in college. I had the nearly impossible job of scouring a large area of dense forest, rich with wetlands and checkered with clear-cut logged areas, in search of finding and monitoring songbird nests.

Ripe with ambition and an impulse to not only prove myself clever, but tough and rugged enough to take on the wilderness, I soon discovered that this was neither an easy nor a very enjoyable task. I encountered mosquitoes on an order of magnitude greater than anything I had imagined existed. Tightly woven clothing and heavy rubber boots were not the best attire for walking miles each day across rough terrain, and they became the worst kind of burden in the heat and humidity. My close encounters with a wolf and then a bear the very next day left this "brave" 21-year-old shaking in her rubber boots and nearly petrified to go back out when the alarm rang at three a.m. the following morning. It was still pitch black when I arrived on site each day, and I'd begin by walking with a flashlight, following pieces of orange ribbon that marked the mile-long transect lines that lead to new places to survey. I frequently felt like I was in uncharted territory, with only a topographic map, a compass, and a whistle for comfort. Modern cell phones didn't exist, and my one work companion was rarely nearby.

Ovenbird nests were among the most difficult to locate. In the half-light before dawn I often found myself moving like a snail across the forest floor, being careful not to step on one of their well-camouflaged nests. When I approached a nest slowly and carefully enough, the female bird would appear... loping and limping with a "broken wing," in an attempt to lure me away from the shelter containing her precious eggs. Each time I discovered one of their nests, I felt a great sense of accomplishment... it was like finding golden treasure buried deep in the jungle. I then enjoyed the privilege of repeatedly visiting the nests to monitor progress... to count the eggs and the hatchlings, and to watch the busy, frazzled parents in their daily routine of raising the young. We shared our lives for a while... the birds and I... and I learned a tremendous amount about patience, tolerance, and acceptance. I learned that things can't be rushed, as I was most successful when I was patient enough to wait and watch. And I learned that the hardships on the dark and scary path can lead to hidden places of intense beauty on the landscape, but only if I keep moving in spite of my fears...

Life moved on after that summer in the forest with the birds. I got married, went to graduate school where I spent more time doing fieldwork, and I eventually became one of those busy and frazzled parents. The woodlands of my childhood finally succeeded in enticing me back home where I began to build my own "nest" on the forest floor. Soon afterwards, I found myself at the end of my 11-year marriage. Several months had passed since my separation and it became evident that my broken record was louder than ever... and now a new face appeared on it. My marriage was over, as well as any hope that I would date this new person, yet the record continued to haunt me, repeating self-defeating thoughts, scenarios, heartache, and lost hope. I yearned to be free... completely free of all the useless thoughts revolving around the romance, drama, and pain. I felt neither tough nor rugged nor brave while facing this wilderness in my mind... I only knew I had to keep moving. I contemplated it for weeks, I journaled about it, I wrote a song about it... and I prayed about it repeatedly.

Then one morning as I sat in my sacred spot outside, I felt a shift... the record began to slow down. I continued to sit in silence, until I was shaken by a loud and sickening "thud" against my dining room window. My heart felt heavy as I stood up and walked around the corner of the house. There, in the grass under the window, lay an Ovenbird... completely motionless... with a broken neck. I picked it up and noticed the brood patch on its stomach... it was a female. Somewhere nearby on the forest floor, there was a nest full of eggs that would not be tended to again. I stood quietly for a while, holding her in my hands, shedding my tears, and praying for her spirit. Then I heard a gentle voice say, "There is great beauty, even in death."...

In that moment... like a flash... I realized the record had stopped. It was as if the turntable had been unplugged... and for the first time I could recall, there was no man living in my head possessing my thoughts. I grieved for the loss of the Ovenbird, and I also felt sadness for the loss of this dysfunctional thought process... It had been a terrible companion, but nevertheless, it had been with me for most of my life. But I was finally free from it... and my tears of grief met with tears of joy, in bittersweet recognition. I carried the Ovenbird to a comfortable place on the forest floor and laid her down. I bid her honor and farewell. And so it was time for me to let go of this other old friend too; it was time to let my old life die, so I could begin a new one... There is great beauty, even in death.

The broken record remained quiet for a long time, and then one day I noticed it spinning again. But because I was given the gift of its silence, I'm no longer afraid to stand up to it and call it what it is... my own creation. It no longer haunts me, it no longer has power over me, and it no longer has any say in what I choose to think or feel... and this, by far, is the sweetest kind of freedom. My ultimate happiness no longer depends on finding a fairytale ending. My ultimate happiness depends on me... and where I focus my thoughts and feelings, and in seeing that each moment holds the power for a new beginning.

I may live my life on the ground in my "nest," but like the Ovenbird, my soul has wings to take me higher... and so it has.

Love Child

It's all right here... closer than you thought;
The hope you've been hoping for,
The wish you've been wishing for,
The love you've been longing for.

Look with your other eyes,
Listen with your other ears,
Feel it with your heart,
As your fingers trace a pathway across the stars.

Can you see the pattern you've sewn together?
Can you hear the repetitive sounds in your head?
You are not these things...

You are made from infinite possibilities
That have come together in a glorious celebration
To dance and sing and make love...

You are a Love Child,
As free as they come.

Soul Food

I wish to talk about love tonight.
In this still air... let's stir things up.

Let's take a cup from each of our souls,
And mix them together.
Then watch what wondrous,
Delicious things transpire.

Forget all your worries and desires,
There is nothing you need.
We have all the ingredients for anything
You could ever want,

So let's learn to cook!

I'll make you my favorite dish,
I'll serve it with the finest wine,

Then we'll eat and tell stories
Until the sun comes up.

My Evening Drink

I open my mouth to drink in this sweet nectar
That sings so brightly
When the night arrives at my doorstep...

An elixir teeming with fruitful silence
And infused with the impressions of
Every thought that has crossed my mind
And every word that has kissed
Or bruised
My lips;

Yet none but the ripe seekers will hear me speak
As I traverse this universe in silent anticipation

Of what will come next...

A season of choice

Yesterday, after talking to a friend about my joys
and trials, she said that I am in a different season
in my life right now, and seasons change.

For a moment tonight as I lay in the dark,
I distinctly felt winter... I had to take a quick breath
to recover from this sensation. Then it felt as though
the bottom fell out of my reality... time no longer
existed... just me and this moment... and then
the next and the next, yet each was the same...

Full of all possibility, full of every season,
and I could choose which one I want to experience.
My life is this choosing one thing or another...
and none is better than or worse than the other,
just different.

I am choosing something every moment.
So what is the picture I choose to paint next,
the story I choose to write... the life I choose to live?

I want to dance with love at my side
and joy in my heart... with grace, with open heart
and open mind and open arms...

Different Eyes

When I look with different eyes,
I see that I already have what I long for.

When I long to be embraced,
I lay down on the soft earth.

When I long to be caressed and kissed,
I step into the air, sometimes gentle and dry,
Sometimes forceful and wet;
But always welcoming, always exciting.

When I long to hear my lover sing,
I listen to the trees swaying and playing in the breeze.

When I long to make love,
I flirt with the life energies around me,
Opening myself more and ever more
To the pulsating flow...
Allowing me to see my wholeness
and connecting me to all that is.

When I feel my love has left me,
I look in my Heart and see that God has not moved
from this precious abode;

It was just I who was looking away
in the other direction.

Middle Age

I wonder if this is the feeling of middle age?
I sense things slipping, shifting,
and moving at a greater pace.
There's a good chance that the rest of my life
will be shorter than what I've already experienced.

I find myself melancholy and deeply emotional
in witness to things I once would have quickly
turned away from without much thought.
I'm seeing life from a broader perspective,
and this brings freedom, and richness, and joy,
and a deeper connection to creation.

There's nothing to fake anymore,
there's nothing to hide,
there's nothing to run away from.
I've seen my biggest demons... and they are me.
I've seen my greatest champion... and it is me.
I've seen the love inside my chest grow and grow,
reaching outward to embrace the whole world.

I've felt my power – I've watched it scatter
when I lose my focus, and I watch it heal me
and my world when I pull it together.

I am strong, and powerful, and abundant.
But I am also humbled, and grateful,
and I'm no longer afraid to let myself fall apart...
to let myself feel and grieve and purge...
to allow life to flow through me like a river...
to let the tears flow like a cleansing rain.

Everything passes, everything shifts,
everything moves... there's nothing to resist...
just let it flow...
And the rain allows the flower
to open more
and ever more...

And ever more.

Capsized

Serenity is the calm that floats gently,
Gently on the waves.
Where peace warms like sunshine
And joy caresses my face.

Where I sit in quiet solitude,
My sails set to soar.
Keeping rhythm with divine forces,
I wait for nothing more.

Turmoil is the cold, cold waters
That lap and rap my head,
That tear and glare and shred my heart
And weigh it down like lead.

So how can it be I've let a hand,
A hand I barely know,
Rock this calm serenity,
Capsizing me head to toe?

Now drenched and cold I tread alone,
To rise above these waves.
And set my sails so peace and joy
Can take me home again.

To Thine Own Heart

Sometimes the things that seem so strong
Are the most fragile.

And you can't go back and re-do
Any more than you can glue
The broken pieces with missing parts
Or fire and forge a brand new heart.

But you can change your thoughts
About pleasure and pain;
You can forge ahead
Seeking rainbows from rain,

So whether or not the sky is blue,
To thine own heart,
Always be true.

Like a Flower

You're like a flower
Growing strong and beautiful.

Don't let anyone pick you
For a vase upon their table;

Whilst they become so disappointed
When you wilt.

Soul Mates

Tonight the rain reminds me,
And the thunder shakes loose memories
From hiding places deep inside my mind.
Deep inside my body
Live the sights and sounds and feelings...
I embrace them once again
As lightening chases the wind.

I close my eyes and see the path ahead,
I feel the soft earth beneath my naked feet...
I can feel you near, watching me
With your thoughtful eyes.
You see my passions and hand me a torch...
Lit from your own heart's fire.

Brighter and brighter it burns as I pull it to my chest,
My heart growing brighter in recognition
Of this flame that burns between us.

How many times we've met on this path,
I do not know; and this time
You're taking your sweet time.
This time you'll come and we'll meet
On the other side of this veil...
And I will know sweet union once again.

When you arrive

For as many times as I've been hurt,
Through the countless tears,
And the endless grief,
I stand before you now.

For as many times that I have fallen,
And got back up
To fall again, and again, and again,
I stand before you now.

Through all the heartache and sorrow,
Through the dark nights
And the darker days,
I stand before you now.

I offer only love,
Because that is what I am made of.
I offer it fully,
From a heart made whole through the journey.

What appeared as my struggles,
Was my preparation for you.

I am here.
When you arrive, I am here.

All that matters

Names do not matter
As I sit in your presence;
Like sitting before God,
Who knows me more deeply than I know myself.

Words do not matter
As we sit in this silence
Full of life and light between us,
Full of unspoken laughter and knowing smiles.

All that matters is here
In this moment,
As eternity unfolds before us,
Beheld in each glance given.

I know you not by your name.
I know you by the light in your eyes,
The gift in your heart,
The smile on your face... offering grace.

And that is all that matters.

Let's do this softly

Softly, softly, softly
The butterfly flutters and lands;
And when one meets another,
They dance, and dance so gently.

Let's do this softly;
And when we meet,
Let's dance, and dance
So gently.

This kind of nourishment

My every breath now calls to you
To move closer and closer to my chest.

My every word now speaks to you
Of the love that burns deep in my heart...
Of the desire that burns white in my soul...
Of the sweet essence of life I taste in your kiss.

So come closer...
Feel the fire I have to warm you,
To inspire you,
To sustain you,
Then take me in your arms and kiss me...

And we'll live forever
With this kind of nourishment.

This Time

Time is not what it used to be.
I refuse to take anything for granted,
There simply is not enough time for that.

I want to take you in
With my eyes and ears and arms and mouth,
And savor your presence right here, right now.

I want to sit with you and talk
Until the sun comes up.
I want to feel your skin on mine,
Your heart divine,

And know you're mine... oh mine,
This time,
This time.

A Thousand Daggers

If a thousand daggers came raining down,
I'd stand with you,
Still stand with you.

If lightning and thunder shook apart
This fragile ground,
I'd lie with you,
Still lie with you.

If floods and famine swept us up
In a tortuous sound,
I'd die with you,
Love, die with you.

So when nothing is left of body or mind,
I'll fly with you,
Become the sky with you;
Our touch, the wind,
Our kiss, where sweet air meets ground,
And our love will grow,
Becoming this whole world.

The Mystery

It's better to not have anyone
Completely figured out.
Do we have God completely figured out?

The mystery is key
To respect and honor.

Don't make assumptions
From your limited perspective,
But understand there is always more...
Forever... more.

Let's make a deal

We were here before
And we'll come again,
Just say the word
And we'll play, my friend.
I'll be up when you are down,
You'll be the sunshine
To warm my ground.
Let's make a deal,
Let's make a bet
That in our hearts
An impression is set...
And I'll know you,
And you'll know me
Next time we meet
In this beautiful
Sweet
Mystery.

Make Love

If you're happy and you know it,
Make love.
If you're frustrated and troubled,
Make love.
If you're out of sorts with the world,
With another,
With your sisters and your brothers,
Make love.
Make love with the world,
Make love with your dreams,
Make love with your other,
Because no matter how it seems,
We came here for this;
Full of piss and sunbeams,
To make love out of nothing,
And from this
Comes everything.

The sweetest things

This silence
That gently brushes across my face
Like a peaceful breeze,

Kisses my lips
And reminds me

That the sweetest things come
When nothing is said.

Air, Earth, and Fire

A time comes when you can't care anymore...
I mean the kind of caring that is like
Trying to control, or fix, or make better.
The kind of caring that leads you to believe
There is a problem to overcome.

You can love someone without that.
You can love them wholeheartedly,
With unconditional acceptance
For them as they are,
For you as you are,
And the world as it is.

Then, and only then, do things move and shift
Into the realm of your wishes and desires,
Turning air, earth, and fire
Into the world you are only just now
Dreaming of.

No Limits

Send out your love to the world...
Send it to those you love,
And send it to those you hate.
Send it to the tree tops
And through the clouds
Right into Heaven's gate.

Send it through storm
And the seas as they swell,
Send it through fire
And ice cold as Hell.

Send it to all,
Lovers and haters,
Makers and breakers,
Honest or fakers.

There are no limits
To your love
There are no limits

To
Love.

Cracked Open

I don't know if you know it,
But you've cracked me open.

I lay here exposed and raw,
Without a shell or outer protection.

I've let you in to see where the darkness dwells,
And the lightness swells,

Chasing out demons
No longer trapped inside

This cage.

Let's get drunk

Let's get drunk on life...
I'm tired of being sober,
I'm tired of being somber,
And straight-laced and proper.

Come grab me by the hips
And pull me close,
And tease me with your hands and lips,
Like you do
When you've been drinking.

Come dance with me
Amidst the chaos and the dirty dishes,
And whisper to me what you hear
While we listen with our hearts wide open,

In God's sweet tavern.

The Journey

to

Wholeness

Spirit Waves

Books have always had a way of "jumping" off the shelf and into my hands when I most need the guidance and advice contained within them. Through the voice of a friend, I find words of inspiration at just the right moment. These things have taught me that synchronicity is a normal and expected part of life. I have learned that if I am patient, the right words, the right situation, the right person will come along and deliver the perfect message. Everything becomes a teacher, the perceived "good" and "bad" alike, the happy moments and the difficult times.

Even the malfunctioning radio in my old jeep became a transducer from spirit to my ears. It had stopped playing regularly years prior; I'm sure the result of a loose connection that was only remedied on moments when I would drive over a big bump or slam my fist down firmly on the dash board. It would then proceed to play until I hit another bump, which would render it silent once again. In the early stages of building my house, any questions I had of whether or not I made the right decision to move back to the woods of my childhood were answered one day by the radio. I had just finished working on the house for the day, and drove away from the construction site with my 4-year-old son in tow. We had just reached the intersection next to my former elementary school, which had since been converted to a bar and grill appropriately named "Boondocks." As I slowed to a stop on the smooth road surface, the radio, which had been silent for days despite my repeated poundings on the dash, suddenly started working. Blaring from the worn-out speakers, I heard a recognizable song from my childhood... "Down in the Boondocks." I was stunned. I looked back at my smiling child and we both started laughing; me at the "coincidental" circumstance and him joining in for the joy of the moment. I stared in wonderment at the old school building now bearing the name of the song that filled our ears; I thought about my childhood here and my life since I moved away, and I saw the perfection of a greater plan tying it all together, even if I didn't understand the details or know the ultimate outcome... then, slowly, I pressed down on the gas pedal. As we crossed the intersection, the radio stopped playing. I was reminded in that one glorious moment that every moment is just that glorious. I only need to be willing to be open to whatever presents itself and to listen to whatever kind of radio that spirit chooses to speak through. Just like radio waves, I think there are spirit waves... speaking to us and offering answers and advice, at all times.

In many ways I am like that radio... a perfect receiver for spirit to speak through, as long as I am properly connected. And depending on the bumps I hit along the way, sometimes I am jarred and shaken, but this has often helped me to be a better receiver. Sometimes the rough spots I experienced have ultimately been just what I needed to help me wake up and start functioning the way I'm meant to work... to be the way I'm meant to be.

One on occasion, shortly after moving back to the Iron Range, I was feeling about as disconnected as I have ever felt. Distraught, anxious, and very sad, I was feeling tremendously lonely. I had recently completed a wonderful weekend of intense spiritual work in a healing arts class, but I was feeling disconnected even from that. I was still adjusting to everything I had learned that weekend and I was working hard to focus my attention and energies for longer and longer periods of time. I knew that if I wanted to pursue this kind of work for myself, if I wanted to live the kind of life that gives more than it takes, while keeping myself replenished, then I could not let this kind of disconnectedness linger; I could not let it suck me in and take my energy. I stepped outside into the fresh air, aching and longing and at a loss as to what to do with everything that I was feeling. I walked across my yard and entered the woods where the red pines and raspberries grow. I walked out, and knew that I could not turn back; I could not go back into my house and continue to wallow in my depression. And I did not carry thoughts of "I'll try," but instead a very strong determination that "I have to do this... This is my life... This is the life I've committed to, and I cannot let these feelings of separation linger in my life." I found a comfortable place to stand among the berries and trees, bare feet in the prickly raspberry bushes. As I had been learning in the healing work I pursued, I let myself open up completely, first making a strong connection with one red pine tree, then another, and another; then I connected with the other plants surrounding me, and from there it exploded outward, touching everything. I felt so connected, so loved, so strong, and so grateful without shrinking back or feeling small. I began sobbing in both joy and in release of my burdens. A Black-capped Chickadee landed on a branch close by and I felt myself speak from within, "Oh my God, this is the life you've given me. I understand now. I don't have to be small for you to love me. I've always known that I have everything I need inside; it's already there, there's nothing missing, there are no gaps. But you see, I forgot how to use it. Like an instrument within, I had forgotten how to play it. I'm learning again... so Thank You. Every step is a prayer... and it's 'Thank you, thank you, thank you. In all my glory... Thank you.'"

I understood then that everything in existence wants communion... to have contact with everything else. It was the reason I felt like something was missing; it was the reason I had been feeling like I needed a man in my life... the contact, the communion, the touching – both physical and emotional. I then saw that the trees want to be touched and caressed too. Everything is reaching out; not in achy longing, but in love and joy and a want of communion. I could see that this is what had been missing in my life. No wonder why we ache in our culture, no wonder why it often feels like something is missing... This is it. Everything in nature is so available... everything is already reaching out. I realized that this connection I have with everything is already there, I just didn't feel it fully before, because I wasn't consciously reaching out myself and asking for the connection. If I make myself as open and available as the trees, the earth, the air, the sun, and I ask for communion, then I am there in that beautiful space where we meet, spirits touching, and I am filled... I am full... full of love, and there is no room for anything less than pure unconditional love for myself and all of creation.

So even after such a profound experience, why don't I live in that beautiful space at all times? Why do I find myself disconnected and distraught on any occasion after having experienced such ecstasy? Life happens, and there is no denying the obligations and stressors that come from working a job with greater responsibility than pay, raising children, doing chores, running errands, doing favors for friends and family in need, coping with health issues, and dealing with interpersonal drama with others in life. There is no denying that these things can cause undue stress. There have been countless times when "just surviving" the day is all I can do, only to start the vicious cycle all over again the very next day. When I am functioning in this kind of survival mode, I become a very bad receiver for spirit. I don't have the time I need for quiet time alone or for pursuing things I truly enjoy. I become like the radio that is silent for days, and I grow weary of hitting bumps when I feel like I have been beaten down too much as it is. I feel like the radio with a loose connection... like a wire separated from the source.

This is the separation... from ourselves, from spirit, from the Universe, from God. But no matter how separated I feel, no matter how far away I feel I have become, whether just a few steps or a million miles, the journey back does not have to be a rigorous struggle nor take a long time. No matter how far away I feel I am, all I need to do is turn around... and I am back. I am back in the center of my being, and in connection and communion with all of spirit, because I was never away from this holy place. Not once have I ever left, nor could I ever leave, for that is not the way it is... That is the real truth. I can only perceive myself as being separated and distanced from a deeper connection with all of existence, and that is the only hell that exists for me. My heaven has always been right here... When I open myself up and listen to the spirit waves, they lead me back to myself and my deep connection with everything... they lead me back to heaven.

Every Sweet Breath

Life is pure, unequivocal joy.
Every thought, word, and deed is sacred,
Every desire of the mind, body, and spirit is sacred...

If I have had anything but a happy heart,
It is because I was without gratitude; without grace,
I allowed fear to drown out life's sweet voice.

That is my choice...
To live in love, or live in fear.
That is my choice...

To live in gratitude for
Every
Sweet
Breath.

You are the Light

You are fervor and power and light.
You have everything within you
To overcome any hardship
Any conflict,
Any situation,
Because you are greater than any situation.
You are greater than anything in existence
That would have you believe
Otherwise.

Overflow

Though my body be weary,
My heart lies wide awake;
Wide awake at dawn and dusk,
Wide awake, full of desire and lust

For what lies ahead,
For what lies within;
I come to you in secret,

Shhhh...

Watch me overflow
From this brim.

Let us not forget

It is because we forget,
If the days are long.
It is because we forget,
If struggles become strong.

It is because we forget...
I see you as wrong,
And myself the only right
In this fight
And I so long;

I so long for peace and rest and song,
I so long to hear the truth
That is gone
To some faraway land
In my mind, it seems lost.

It is because we forget,
That we pay this cost.
So remind me, remind me, remind me,
Dear light,
That I'm not here to put up a fight,
And you're not wrong
And I'm not right.

We are breath and dance and song and light,
We are mirrors and echoes of truth and love
And clear, clean sight,
We are beacons of hope,
Here to ignite

The flame that burns in every soul,
The love that shines and makes us whole.
So throw down the sword and false defense,
Throw down the robe of your pretense.

Let us not forget,
Let us not forget.

Misery loves company

Misery loves company,
It's trying to snuggle up next to me,
To make its home in my happy head,
To follow me up and back to bed;

To dine with me by candlelight,
To wallow in sorrow by pale moon light,
To struggle and lose every impending fight,
I have not strength to carry such strife;

I have not want nor need for it,
I have no way to house this shit,
It reeks of death and loss and spite,
I take a deep breath...

Recover my life.

Faith

Lamenting in my despair,
I cry out for the injustice done;
Asking for reason to give me an answer,
For which I know there is none.

Blinded by my questions,
I have no solace for my grief;
But faith hath wings that carry me
Above all futile belief;

To my true home,
Wherein lies a throne
Upon which my soul takes seat...

And doubt is never a thief.

Old Clothes

We believe what we choose to believe.
Like a closet full of old, comfortable clothes,
We often choose the same things over and over
Without much consideration.

Maybe we should try running around naked,
In order to see
The truth.

The Harder Way

One thing I've learned...
The world is in need of love,
But sometimes it's not the mushy gushy
Love everyone and everything
And then it'll all be better love.

Sometimes it's harder love.
Sometimes it's standing up for what's right
And putting up a fight
When you get sucker punched
Or someone you love gets sucker punched.

Sometimes it hurts your knuckles
And hurts your stomach,
But at the end of the day,
You stand in a better place,
Because you took the harder way.

You will see me fight

When injustice is done,
When selfishness is king,
And daggers of words spill forth
To tell a story untrue;

I will rise up and fight,
With sword in hand,
Pen in palm,
To speak the truth.

And while my way
Has been one of peace,
And my preference
Is for calm...
Still...
Silence...
I will not sit idly by.

I will raise this sword
And defend
What is right
And just
And good
In this world.

For I have come here
For many reasons;
And in the right season,
You will see me fight, my Dear,
You will see me fight.

And when this battle is over,
The king of truth will reign
Strong in my heart;
Burning
Straight
Through
The darkest night.

The Earth's Womb

Sometimes we need to burrow deep down inside,
And surround ourselves with blankets of silence;

And like a dark, quiet womb,
Allow the Earth to comfort us.

Beware the Ghosts

Someone else's baggage
Can be so temping to pick up,
When we are trying to be helpful
And they seem so out of luck.

A shiny bag of secrets
Can look colorful and new,
But beware the ghosts that harbor it
May say they belong to you.

Becoming Whole

At some point, everything comes out into the light.
If it is not made of pure light, for your higher good,
it will not survive.

But don't be surprised if it puts up a hard fight.
Anything you've ever put any energy into,
anything you've created, is not unlike a living entity.
One that will fight to stay alive, in its exact form,
for whatever purpose you intended for it.

So grant it the gratitude it deserves,
give thanks for whatever purpose it had,
whether or not it ever served any real good,
and kiss it farewell.

Then take the energy back to your core, nurture it
well, and be careful how you choose to use it next.
Everything we think, say, and do is medicine.
It can heal us, or it can poison us.
So choose your medicine wisely.

And allow the light to crack you open
and pour into the dark corners and hidden places
and make you whole once again...

It might sting and burn
like antiseptic on your wounds,
but it is the only way to heal, to feel...
To become whole.

Forgiveness

I can't keep hating like this.
I'm not built for it.
Burning hot,
Fierce fire within,
This smoke I can't see through.
I lose myself
And become only
A figure of disdain
In their world.
My life is worth
Infinitely more than this
Transparent
Fruitless
Endless abyss.
Forgiveness screams out
To wake me up,
Shake me up,
"Don't give in to this!
I have news for you,
My dear.
I am not here to
Make anyone right;
I am here to save you,
Never degrade you.

So hold my hand
And I will carry you through
This dark night;
Just me and you
And God's loving,
Gracious light."

Anger

Does anger have a place in my body and my heart,
To turn and churn
And tear things apart,
To melt things down
So I can make a new start?

Yes, sometimes I let it in,
With passion or pain
Or patience worn thin;

I let it pass through,
I let it pass on,
Because anger is not something
Meant to hold for long.

Like hot burning embers
In the palm of my hand,
It destroys heart and flesh,
Turning castles into sand.

Release

I release everything that is not mine;
I release my worries and fears,
And those that belong to others.

I release the need to control circumstances
In my life and in the lives of others.
I am greater than any circumstance;
I rise above the struggles and strife.

I accept everything as it is
Right here, right now.
I am free and I am complete;

I allow peace and prosperity into my heart
To dwell forevermore.

Love is what I've got

Some days are so darn easy,
And some days are definitely not;
But without the struggles
How would I know
That love is what I've got.

This fortune can't be bought
Or sold
For all the gold,
And I've been told
It's worth more anyway
Than anything else
That would come my way.

So welcome struggle
And welcome strife,
Welcome into my world,
Into my life;
Let's sit for a while,
Just you and I...

And talk about the weather.

What am I afraid of?

What am I afraid of?
These cells in my body that don't belong?
What am I afraid of?
The cutting of tissue to rid my body
Of these unwelcomed guests?
What am I afraid of?
Getting weak and sicker if this doesn't succeed?
What am I afraid of?
Death?

And I realize... NO,
These are not things to be afraid of.
My fears stem only from an unknown fate.
Death and Destiny wrapped together,
One cannot be without the other.

So I wrap my arms around both;
And say, "You are welcome here,
You are my end and my beginning,
You are my driving force,
You are the pointer of my way,
And when the time is right some fateful day,
I will meet you both together."

Life just rushes in

There is no need to worry.
Life just rushes in and fills up the gaps.

It is said

It is said
That in the moment of your death,
All things fall away
And you see what is most important;
You see what is worth living for.

So die.
I tell you, die right now!
Die to your Self...
Why wait for your body to go first?

Why wait for old age to wear you down?
Why wait for anything at all?
Let it all fall away,
Let it all fall away.

There is nothing to fear...
So lighten this load
And brighten the road
So you can walk with Life in your chest
And Purpose in your Heart.

Just for you

Life is not about over-extending,
And giving more and more
Until your resources run out.

Life is about feeling the joy of who you are;
It is about sharing that joy,
And extending a hand to others in a way
That multiplies that joy for everyone involved.

You are not obligated to do anything.
Do not allow feelings of guilt or worry
To crowd out the voice in your heart;
The one that calls to you
To follow your bliss, to follow the path
That only you can walk;
The one that God has silently laid before you,
Just for you...
Just for you...

Your joy being your compass and guide,
Pointing you in the right direction.

Persistence

Persistence is what life is full of.

Full, like the flower in full bloom;
Like the river that overflows its banks,
Its boundaries;
And in turn for this drowning,
The valley is replenished and nourished
And renewed.

Full, like the beauty of the setting sun,
Sending out fireballs of vibrant color;
Filling the sky,
Filling my eyes
Till I'm glowing and flowing with ecstasy.

Stay on this path,
And you will find your nourishment.

Stay on this path,
And beauty will follow you.

The Greatest Choice

People don't do bad things to you because of you;
They do bad things to you because of themselves.
As well, people do good things for you
Because of themselves.

So in every relationship we have,
Whether we see it as good or bad,
We have an opportunity to choose
Who we want to be.

And when a friendship or any relationship ends,
We could blame the other person
For any number of things;
But in the end, it ended
Because it did not support the person
You chose to be.

In the light of truth,
All falsities fall away,
So don't grieve this loss too long...
Celebrate the extra room
You now have in your heart
To give yourself the love and honor you deserve.

Stand strong in who you are,
Stand strong in the light of truth.
The greatest choice
Is choosing you.

Traveling on

Have you heard the geese
When they fly at night?
Traveling on,
Traveling on.

Have you felt the wind
Blowing with all its might?
Traveling on,
Traveling on.

Have you seen the moon
Trace a pathway across the sky?
Traveling on,
Traveling on.

The spirit is that way,
Its movement ever light.

Let it carry us across the sky,
Let it call to us...

And never wonder why
It's traveling on,
Traveling on.

This Game

I step with one foot,
And then the other...

Until I stand firmly on this changing ground,
My mind inviting peace
Regardless of the chaos that surrounds;

Until I know the path by way of my heart,
And each day,
Another chance to start,
Another chance to choose.

And the very best part of this wonderful game
Is that I get to play;
I thank God I get to play!

And by doing so,
There is no way to lose.

Hit the gas

The world WILL get crazier.
Things will fall apart
Before they fall together.

Blessings come in disguises;
Call it what you may,
Naming only goes so far...

See the truth under the ashes,
Burned clean and bright
Despite the dirt that covers it.

Life was meant to be LIVED.
I said LIFE was meant to be LIVED.

So stop the bullshit baby whining,
Stop the moping
And the doping yourself up,
Stop the crap you fill your head up with,
Stop the nonsense,

And start to live,
And start to live,
And start to live...

Hit the choke,
Hit the gas,
And go, baby,
Go...

Defer to God

There comes a point
When all the fight
Is gone.

When all the right
And wrong
And weak
And strong
Become the same
Gray
Blur;

The same
Lame
Energy sapping game,
As it were.

This is when
I defer
To God.

Some may look
And see defeat,
To others it appears
A turn of cheek,
A white flag thrown,
To wherever the wind has blown;

But I tell you a secret,
This makes you no less,
Or more weak
In spirit or heart
In distress.

There is wisdom hidden
Within this key,
There is joy to be had
Whether you protest
Or agree;

There is nothing
You need to do,
Dear soul...

Just

Be.

Let it be

Healing is an opening to all possibility.

It is allowing yourself to be who you truly are,
And to be happy.

It's that simple.

Just let it be.

God and the farmer

Come,
Rest your head on my lap,
And I will give you a drink
Called Peace.

Sometimes,
We all just need
A little reprieve.

I will tell you a story
About God and the farmer,
About the Earth
And the Sun
And their heated love affair.

And if I don't have you smiling;
If I don't have you wondering
What this is all about,
Then I'll give you
The whole bottle,
And at least tonight
You will get
Some good rest.

Gratitude

The key to peace and happiness lie in gratitude.
When I practice gratitude, the world shifts,
And what I thought was unmovable, moves,
What I thought was unattainable, I gain.

When I am thankful for every breath,
Every star, every grain of dirt under my feet,
Every creature, every plant, every drop of water,
Every beat beat beat of my heart;

When I am thankful for every right
And every wrong,
For all who have hurt me and all who have helped,
For all who love and all who hate,
For myself in all my moods
And calamities and mistakes;

When I am thankful for it all,
Even my separation from myself and divine light,
I surrender every strife, every hurt,
Every longing I hold,
And I'm left with just me...

Just me and the world,
And suddenly,
That is enough...
That is everything.

Dancing with God

In the quiet stillness of my heart,
I go to seek solitude.

But the peace I find is far from lonely,
For when I arrive,
There is an ancient fire;

And like a moth to a flame,
I am drawn to spread my wings
And dance, and dance
With God.

Sweet   Dreams

Sweet dreams, sweet lies, sweet lovers in disguise.

Take off the mask and bare your soul,
If you dare to dream of something whole;

If you dare to step into the dark,
And trust, Dear One, trust

Your Heart.

About the author

Kate Ingrid Paul is an energy healing practitioner and organic farmer. Growing up in a down-to-earth rural environment, receiving a Master's Degree in Biology, and farming have kept her hands and feet close to the earth, while her experiences and encounters of a mystical nature have cultivated her sacred perspective on life. Her heart felt writings weave together the natural world with a more magical one, in an ecstatic celebration of life. She lives "Down in the Boondocks" with her husband and family.

Her websites are owlforesthealing.com and owlforestfarm.com.

Made in the USA
San Bernardino, CA
23 November 2013